Listening for Low Tide

poems

James P. Cooper

Choeofpleirn Press ~ Leavenworth, Kansas
2026 Edition

Copyright © 2022 Choeofpleirn Press

Cover Photo by James P. Cooper; first published in *Red Moon Cafe*

Choeofpleirn Press

Leavenworth, KS 66048
choeofpleirnpress@gmail.com
www.choeofpleirnpress.com

ISBN: 979-8-218-11188-5

Table of Contents

Under a Dark Sky

Miles from the nearest
cluster of houses, whose lights
confuse the migrating moths,

we park next to a field, hear
the swish of cows, their dark shapes
moving toward the fence

as you mount your camera
on its tripod in the gravel road.
We wait. Cows wander away.

Throat singing, frogs perform
their songs of lust, daring us
to add our song, until you cry out

at meteors. Their bright tails swim
across each shot, their getting
pulled inside exhausts them.

Gust Front

Its crown three stories high,
the elm in my yard overlooked
fields once planted in corn grow
crowded with houses. Its limbs hollow,
it dropped branches onto my car,
forcing me to drive out from camouflage.

One night in July, the thunder,
still remaining to the north, idling,
brought me outside to move my car.
I saw the wind rushing toward me,
cleaning the street ahead of it, driving
dust and litter to the sides. Running,
I headed for the porch as limbs began

cracking, as a flurry of leaves landed
in the street, the yard, as the sign
on the corner stuttered and shook.
I stopped and saw my car supporting
a branch like a sawhorse, its right side
crushed, the windshield a scattering
of corn spilled during harvest.

Those Nights

Nearly any summer night,
when I step outside to feed the strays,
could be a good one, once again,

for standing at the nose
of a KC-135 loaded with fuel,
nothing but prairie in the darkness
outside the fence line. Shipped overseas,
I guarded three nuclear bombs,

each one attached to the jet fighters
parked in their bright hangars,
both ends open, while I slouched
in my dark gate shack, the door open,
my feet propped up, with nothing
to occupy my head but the sensation

of listening to the radio tucked
in my clothes; the music, rising and fading
like an engine on the run-up pad,
ended at 2:00 a.m., six hours before
a pick-up truck dropped off my relief.

At War with Darkness

I stepped down from the train
at nearly midnight. Located three miles
from the village but twelve miles from the airbase,
the station saw traffic only on weekends.

The other people got in the cars waiting
for them and passed me as I started walking
toward the lights of the village. Newly arrived
from the States, I knew no one and had
no one to call. No streetlights lined the road.
Behind clouds, the moon and stars provided
no help. The cat's eyes in the road remained shut.

After the village, I started walking
through nine miles of darkness, its curtain
pulled shut behind me. The hedges along
the road separated me from fields of sugar beets.

Trees seemed to link their limbs above me,
creating a tunnel through which I had
to continue walking. Someone or something
was watching me, but no one jumped out;
no animal ran in front of me. I heard
no sounds but for my own footsteps.

I missed the short cut that ran in front
of the approach lights. As I reached
the crossroads and took the road leading
to the airbase, I saw the curtain
slowly slide open. Over the next year,

I spent nights guarding planes against what
a double row of chain link fence and lights
above the fence line worked to repel.
I carried that war against darkness home
with me. Although the bedroom curtain,
tacked at its edges, blocks all light,
I cannot sleep in total darkness. Two lights
shield the room from what might lurk close-by.

Union Pacific

Stillwater, Oklahoma

I miss hearing freight trains.
Two engines shift cars along
this spur on Thursdays and Sundays.

Trains ran to and from the yard
on two tracks alongside the river
in Kansas City. Their horns, like chimes,
broke up each hour, reminding me
of the motion going on around me--
gondolas carrying coal from Wyoming,
autos shipped west across Kansas,
containers stacked on top of each other
brought in on flatcars from California,

On my porch at night, I unwrap
bundles pulled from storage, sift
through those places strung together
like paper dolls and connected by horns.

Sitting Alone, Listening

Since Montana, I have come to know nights
divided by sound, beginning with trains
wailing as they slide through town,
their cries clogging the air like smoke
as they are pushed toward the Rockies.

I heard trains in England switching lines
and clacking over rails at 2:00 a.m.
Foghorns in San Francisco carried
the sound of cows grazing in a far pasture,
as though boats churn the ground in Kansas,
where in five towns I have heard trains
rise through the night and blow like whales
before diving back into farmland. On Adak,

an island next to a volcano venting steam,
silence broke when tremors shook the ground
like four diesels coupled together
and pulling a hundred cars into the sea.

Nightfall at Boomer Lake

Alone, still sitting in the car,
the engine off, the window open,
a hundred years after the Boomers
left Kansas to lay claim to land
in Indian Territory, I stare across

the water of this manmade lake, hear
the wintering geese before eight
of them glide onto the far shore.
Great egrets summered here last year,
feeding along the shore across

the road, but roosting at dusk
on limbs that leaf out every year,
the drowned trunks close enough
to shore for these birds to appear
in detail, all five facing north

in my photos. I no longer look
northwards toward my last home.
These lights on the eastern shore
mirror Kansas City from the bluffs
above the Kansas River, resemble

Ireland, the castle and town
of Carrickfergus, when riding
the ferry from Belfast to Stranraer
or standing in Bangor across the lough.
I carry these places inside of me.

At the Airport in Pratt, Kansas

We are parked at the airport,
both doors open to the summer night.
A warm wind buffets the car.

We watch the red and white lights
revolving on top of the water tower.
A green light shows up, too,
you say, but my eyes cannot see

that color. No one flies overhead.
No one follows this beacon shooting
across fields like a searchlight.
You point out the light bulbs strung
along the edge of the feedlot, where cows
have been corralled since autumn.

I hear their cries. I imagine
they are now protesting a roundup,
their rumps raw from prods
as they are crowded into trucks.

You sit on the hood and stare overhead
at the stars, looking for Perseus.
I hear only the tractor trailers
headed west, hauling cows to Dodge City
and the slaughterhouse.

Stenciling Another Kill

When I see the bodies of opossums,
raccoons, and deer alongside the road,
I am reminded of the career NCO
who used to run down rabbits at night.

Assigned to the team always ready
for emergencies, I rode with this sergeant.
Mid-shift, about 4:00 a.m., he parked
his pick-up on the flight line, with lights off.

After a half-hour, he flipped on his lights
and targeted both adults and children.
I sat in silence, grimacing, when he started
laughing and turned to see whether I enjoyed
hearing the thud under his tires.

The number of kills if stenciled on his truck,
would have taken up not just
the driver's door but that entire side.

Maybe like Sisyphus, his punishment never
ends as he gets reincarnated as a rabbit
at the moment it attempts to outrun and evade
capture by zig-zagging in front of a truck.
None of its attempts ever lead to safety.

Memorial Day

Pratt, Kansas

The barn door slamming shut
loosened hundreds of moths--
millers to us. My niece and nephew
called me outside to hunt for them.
We threw open the door of the shed.
Already leaning southward, its walls
folded in like cards, sending a cloud
of millers above our heads. We dislodged
more by opening the hoods of cars
parked in the yard, jumped back
as millers burst out like confetti.
That night their bodies knocked
against the windows, the dusty imprints
of their bodies left on the glass.
A dozen more barged in each time
we opened the door. Our cat, batting
them onto the floor, snacked at first,
then left their carcasses littering
the rug, as if she were shooting
buffalo from a train in Kansas. Outside,
squatters, who had squeezed past
the rubber seals at the doors,
escaped when I packed the car
the next afternoon. That night,
in Kansas City, with the garage
door open, the lights off, I opened
the trunk, saw millers break
for the streetlights, a dozen ghosts
haunting the air above our house.

A Monday Night in Late July

I have loved my wife to sleep.
She moans softly and rolls over,
wrapping an arm around my pillow,
as I leave our bed and dress
in shorts and a shirt left unbuttoned.

Our cats sprint after moths
let inside while I wheel my bicycle
out the door. Everyone else sleeps
on a Monday night in late July.
The streets are mine. I pedal and coast,

letting the air cool my skin.
I circle the downtown sprinklers,
splashing through puddles and breaking
the reflections of flashing red traffic lights.

Katydids record the number
of stars visible overhead as I turn
toward home. When I climb into bed, my wife
greets me by throwing a leg over mine.

Kneeling in Prayer

I dropped part of my car outside
Enid, Oklahoma, along U.S. 64.
My mechanic gives it, maybe,
another year. The rust peels off
paint and crunches through the frame.

My bank account spits out mud
whenever I lift the handle and try
to fill the sink. If I only knew
what to awaken, I would sing sweetly,
like droplets of rain, offering a song
each morning, afternoon, and evening.

My only tree, a twenty-year-old cottonwood,
whose limbs shaded my window,
and whose seeds floated past like moths,
dirtying the neighbor's yard, was cut down
last summer when she complained
to the town. Nothing else covers me

but the sky. My landlord releasing
the coolant from the air conditioner
lets its cancer spread to clouds
and gnaw holes over Antarctica.

Maybe I should lie down next to you,
placing my ear over your stomach,
to hear a forest waking in your body.
The afternoon school bells drifting
over the town call us now into prayer.

October in Oklahoma

I hold out my son's wand
in front of me, wait to catch
that next gust, wait for bubbles
to explode like a water balloon.

Some of them run low along
the ground, dodging the weeds
that need trimmed one last time
this season; others climb the air,
dancing over the neighbor's house.

My son, on the step below mine,
dips his wand in the saucer,
shakes off the droplets that land
in his hair, on his lips, that smear
the porch, my glasses. Nests
deserted by webworms roll across
the yard. Leaves dropped early
collect in the fence like messages
for those others to go down flaming.

A hundred years ago, a cold front
would have rushed past, its gusts
twisting the windharp hung in a tree,
giving voice to spirits warned
away by bonfires, to the dead warming
themselves in our houses, feeding
themselves against the coming cold.

Windchimes, for us, record the front
moving south, as though horses lug
it behind them, their bells ringing.

Snow piles along roads like straw
in Kansas, Nebraska, South Dakota.

Flying Kites with Icarus

Afraid to let my kite flap
more than eight feet above
my head, I pull back
on the string, spooling it
around my hand. Not trained,

still, my falcon stays close
to my gloved hand. My son
unrolls more of his line, seeking
a wind three hundred feet aloft,
encouraging his kite to fight

its line, to join those geese
seemingly inside a wind tunnel,
their wings arched, their bodies
remaining still, their voices faint.
He dares his kite to break free

and surge forward for an instant
before it drifts across a road,
trailing its line like spider silk,
and settles onto electrical lines,
overhanging all five like filigree.

My Father's Deafness

My dad, no matter how much
he cranks the volume, asks me
to talk louder. He ends up saying
he'll get my news from mom
before he hands her the phone.

He used to play with his hearing
aids at dinner, cupping a hand
over each one until it whistled
but much softer than his own
when he used to step outside
before dinner and whistle me home
as if he was still the bo'sun
mate piping the officers aboard ship.

Removing his hearing aids at night,
he sleeps undisturbed, no matter
how loud he snores next to my mom.
Going deaf, I think, would free me
from the noise of my neighbors,
whose stereo at 3 a.m. seems to roar

with the boasting of Zulu tribesmen
rapping their spears against
their shields, their rhythmic motions
meant to frighten the British troops
in a movie my dad once said
captures the essence of discipline.

Jack hammers and chain saws
would stop invading my afternoons.
I wouldn't know when cars, throbbing
with noise, pause at the corner,
force panes to pulse in their frames.
Early Saturday mornings in March,
when fetching the newspaper
from the yard, I would miss flickers

drilling at evergreens, a downy
woodpecker tapping a rhythm
on the chimney, a snare drum
for its rolls, or robins and cardinals
in the magnolia above the feeder,
berating me for not filling it earlier—
just some of the creatures, my dad
writes, that mime their actions for him.

Latching onto Treasure

I stop for the geese flying low.
Their voices assure the leader of their formation
as I leave the car in the parking lot.

Before I discovered the songs
of flickers and cardinals, before I cursed
the neighbors whose dogs kept me from sleeping,
I let music from two midrange speakers,
drive away the family from the rental
house next to mine. Choosing to read

what people are saying, I keep the volume
on the TV low. I insert earplugs
before mowing and use a broom
to collect grass clippings from the driveway.

After I shower, the noise
in my ears sounds like 5,000 snow geese
nestled together. It can take hours
before these geese start to migrate north.
Hundreds remain behind throughout the year.

Listening for Low Tide

Too much happens at ground level:
the kids selling candy or delivering
newspapers shortcut through the yard,
the neighbors' dogs blare their alarms
in unison, and teens, shielded by the heartbeat
of their music, speed down the street.

Two stories above the ground.
I welcome the afternoon sunlight
as it stretches across the rug,
my cat moving with it. From the opposite
window, the shadows cast by trees
overspread the ground, the sunlight only
hitting the treetops. Sound waves lap
against the building, the tide at its lowest
each night when the owl in the park
starts to hoot its presence.

That Silver Cord

Too far out on the pier,
where the wind shifts direction,
sometimes ceasing between gusts,
I struggle to keep my kite
above water. It loops. It dips
a hundred feet in front of me,
nearly providing a cover for fry
against a great blue heron waiting
for their movement, before I tug back

on the string, keeping the kite afloat
until the nylon ripples in another surge
of wind. It seems as if I fly my soul,
controlling it with a string held
at my chest. It tugs at my arms,
daring me to unwind all five
hundred feet, to have it climb

to the height of geese navigating
dusk over the lake, warning others
to move aside. Given too much string,
my kite plunges. I work it toward shore.
I send it aloft again, letting the air
dry its wings and flake off the mud
staining them with a silhouette.

Finding Faith on K-5

Leavenworth to Wolcott

Driving blind, I grip the wheel,
slowing through turns and sprinting
along straightaways, keeping the middle
line to the left. Out of the fog,

taillights might glow moments
before they shatter; cars taking wide turns
might drift into my lane, giving me
seconds to move to the shoulder;
deer might be paused in the road,
listening to my engine approach.

Hurrying to work, I keep descending
onto the floodplain of the Missouri River,
certain that the road remains empty,
that my car continues to break through fog,
that nothing else can keep me
from the highway encircling Kansas City.

An Island in a Sea of Grass

after W.B. Yeats' "The Lake Isle of Innisfree"

On Sunday, while cleaning out pots
on the porch and planting flower seeds,
I thought I was attending an air show.
The cars, accelerating along the street,
seemed to be taking off and flying
low over the crowd, each one trailing
a cloud of white smoke. If I could go
now to somewhere more peaceful,

it would be a house set back
from a gravel road with no neighbors
within shouting distance. From April
to September, the trees surrounding part
of the house would shelter birds
that, every morning, create a choir
of woodwinds. The back porch would offer
an open view of the setting sun,
the light lingering for more than an hour,
even when the sun moves to the south
in winter. My camera and tripod
would be just inside the door
for when clouds dampen the sunset,
reducing it to red and yellow coals.

I am reminded of this place each time
I glimpse the smoldering sky
or when I retreat inside to escape
the noise of traffic taking to the air.

A Postcard from Northern Ireland

Two boys in Bangor face
the Long Hole, a shelter for boats
against weather that sweeps
into Belfast Lough from the Irish Sea.
One boy sits on the concrete rim,
fishing the water that separates
him from three boats tied together,
no tackle box or bucket nearby.
His younger brother, standing
beside him, imagines himself sailing
past the mountains at Newcastle.

Children play tag on the seawall.
Their voices carry to the houses
that line the front, facing
a wash of blues as the lough meets
the sea and the sky. These boys,
for twenty-odd years, have been mailed
to America, Australia, Zimbabwe,
South Africa. They both moved
to Aberdeen, then London for jobs.
Their children find ways to fill
two weeks at St. Ives every summer.

Every Christmas, these brothers
fly home to Belfast, their children
eager to see grandmother, whose house
on Beechfield Street was razed
after a bomb exploded four doors away.
Her new house overlooks Harland
and Wolff, the two yellow cranes,
shaped like dolmens, enclosing
where grandfather welded plates
onto the hulls of freighters.
Every half-hour, their children
hear the train leaving for Bangor,

where I once stood at the end
of Maxwell Lane, watching clouds
drop over the lough, the spray
of the sea mixing with the drizzle
blown into my face, separating me
from the lights of Carrickfergus
across the lough. A ship, waiting
to cross the Irish Sea, dropped
its anchor, as shoppers hurried
home with sausages and wheaten bread
for dinner, before I wrote out,
"Wish you were with me at the folks',"
mailing it to a friend in Kansas.

Siren Song

Sitting beside me
after dinner, my wife
surprises me when she lifts
her shirt and flips up
her bra, telling me
she has crumbs on her boobs.
Cradling her breasts,
she reminds me how warm
and how soft they are.
"Don't you want to touch them,"
she says. Ensnaring me
as if with their song, her breasts
make me into a fisherman
who has lost control of his rudder
and becomes marooned
on the rocks close to the shore.

Love Among Trees

My neighbor once knocked on my door
to tell me that my ash tree dropped
a limb in her yard. More than a hundred
years old and as tall as a signal tower,
this ash tree had no defense against
the ash borer--an alien species. I stayed
awake during storms, dreading that crack
that comes before the tree falls into the house.

Once hired, the tree trimmer waited until October,
after the tree lost its leaves, and after its sap
slipped back into its trunk, to have his crew
saw off the remaining limbs. Their saws
kept us from hearing the tree sighing
as each limb fell. Part of the trunk remains
as a memorial. I imagine that its sap trickled
through the ground and pooled like water
near the roots of its mate located in the yard,
providing a reserve against month-long droughts.

Autumn at Weston Bend State Park

You stand posed in front of me,
one hand gripping your walking stick,
the other hand resting on your hip.

You are smiling at me as I take one picture
after another. The dead leaves, some colored
red, yellow, orange, or brown, collect
on both sides of the dirt path like a foreign
currency. A sign along the pathway asks
that we not pocket the flora. Afternoon shadows
move like strings coming to rest, each one
getting longer as the note fades away.

We are older now, the gray running
like filaments through your brown hair,
my head bare, my face wrinkled.

We never knew to visit this place
years ago when the swollen river
below the bluff ran as brown as the outside
of the house we rented. Our pockets empty,
our passports expired, we are together
as the ground darkens, as the air grows quiet.

Squinting in the Morning Sun

My nights guarding planes on alert
reset my clock. I struggled to relearn sleeping
at night. I lost day jobs because no alarm clock

could wake me. I now set my hours and work
from home. My wife joins me in staying awake
until the shift workers down the street start
their cars at 4:00 a.m. Almost monthly,
over a week's time, before we return to old ways,
we move our hours forward. By day five,

I am walking out to the mailbox at midnight,
the streetlights keeping me from seeing
but a few stars over the neighbors' dark houses.
This past May we were rising as the fireflies
in the park sparked with lust. This October,
as I remember those friends who died at this time

ten years ago, I want to rise early enough to squint
in the morning sun, to picnic beside the trees
along the river, to see the late afternoon sunlight angle
through the neighbor's tree two doors down,
its leaves shining as shadows stretch out their arms,
dousing the light hitting the grass.

Notes

"Memorial Day" records a particularly large infestation of miller moths, the adult stage of the army cutworm. These miller moths migrate to the mountains of Colorado from Kansas and other nearby states during late spring/early summer and often become food for grizzly bears.

"Kneeling in Prayer" is based on Denise Lardner Carmody's description of the Mbuti people in the Iture rainforest in her book *The Oldest God*: *Archaic Religion Yesterday and Today*.

"October in Oklahoma" alludes to the beliefs held by the Celts at Halloween, as described in Sir James George Frazer's *The Golden Bough*.

Acknowledgements

Grateful acknowledgement to the following publications where some of these poems have appeared, sometimes in slightly different form.

Apple Valley Review: "Those Nights"

Connecticut Review: "Kite Flying with Icarus"

Dragon Poet Review: "Gust Front"
                          "October in Oklahoma"
                          "That Silver Cord"

Flint Hills Review: "At the Airport in Pratt, Kansas"

Oklahoma Anthology 1996: "Nightfall at Boomer Lake"

Poetica Review: "Under a Dark Sky"
                      "Stenciling Another Kill"

Project for a New Mythology: "Union Pacific"

Red Rock Review: "Kneeling in Prayer"

Talking River Review: "Love Among Trees"

I want to thank my friend Derick Burleson for his help with some of these poems.

I want to thank my son Harland Cooper for teaching me to look closely, with fresh eyes, at those things nearby.

Most of all, I want to thank my wife Ruth Heflin for her continued support and encouragement, often when it had been a long time since I had last written a poem. Many of these poems would not have been written without her at my side.

About the Author
James P. Cooper

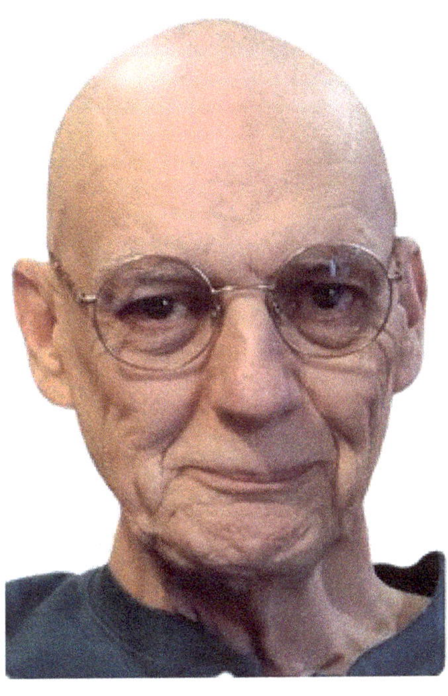

As a Navy brat, James P. Cooper lived in five other countries and two states before the age of eighteen. Beginning at the age of twenty-one, he decided to make his home in Kansas, never having visited the place previously, and although he left the state to live elsewhere on several occasions, he returned to Kansas each time. An AWP Intro Award winner and Pushcart nominee, he has had poems appear in *Apple Valley Review*, *Connecticut Review*, *Flint Hills Review*, *Red Rock Review*, and other journals. He earned a PhD in English from Oklahoma State University, teaches writing online, works as a poetry editor, and blogs occasionally at https://www.redmooncafe.blogspot.com. He lives with his wife, Ruth, and two cats in Leavenworth, Kansas.

See more writing and photos by James P. Cooper at:

James Cooper's *Listening for Low Tide* is a collection of poems that keeps us listening for the sound of a limb breaking from a beloved tree, for train whistles cutting through the night, engines revving, and neighbors next door. These poems take us from overseas "where I guarded three nuclear bombs" to Northern Ireland where the poet writes a postcard to a friend back in Kansas, to an airport is Pratt, Kansas where he watches penned cattle surely bound for slaughter. The images in these poems are clear, fresh, and photographic, sometimes tinged with loss, other times with love. I am reminded of two other poignant Midwest voices, William Stafford and Ted Kooser, who pay attention to the things most of us miss and bring them to us as gifts of language. In Cooper's poem, "Memorial Day," we encounter hundreds of moths, "millers to us," with a kind of delightful specificity that has us batting at them like the cat, "ghosts haunting the air above the house." These poems will haunt you in a good way, like the millers, letting loose the ghosts of people, places, and events stuffed away in the trunk of memory.

Anita Skeen
Series Editor, Wheelbarrow Books
Founding Director, Michigan State University Center for Poetry

---

The poems in this volume listen as much as they speak. The voices of frogs, geese and katydids coexist with the sounds of jackhammers, chainsaws and trucks bound for slaughterhouses. As such, there is a gentle, pastoral quality that overlays the subtle urgencies of potential violence and destruction. These core tensions are ever present and well-wrought in Cooper's thoughtful poems.

Mark Cox
Author of *Readiness* and *Sorrow Bread*

In *Listening for Low Tide*, the further, more distant tide without which nothing continues, James Cooper moves the reader through a deceptively quiet, sometimes lonely world. At times, the poems offer an understated spookiness where a man alone puts into words things so large that only offering the small things of a life may offer clarity. Cooper's poems also are lovingly threaded with an interior music.

Pamela (Jody) Stewart
author of *This Momentary World: Selected Poems*

The Jonathan Holden Poetry Chapbook Contest was an annual competition for poets who have not yet published a chapbook or full-length collection of poems.

Choeofpleirn Press will begin holding a new contest, the **Poetry Book Contest**, for full length poetry collections by poets who have not yet published a full-length book in January 2027.

The Kenneth Johnston Nonfiction Book Award was an annual nonfiction book contest sponsored by Choeofpleirn Press, but which has been discontinued.

In September 2026, Choeofpleirn Press will begin hosting the Ben **Nyberg Short Fiction Collection Contest**.

See our website for submission guidelines for our contests: www.choeofpleirnpress.com.

Also available from Choeofpleirn Press

Poetry:
Amy Lerman's *Orbital Debris,* Winner of Jonathan Holden Poetry
    Chapbook Contest, 2022
Fran Schumer's *Weight,* Finalist of Jonathan Holden Poetry
    Chapbook Contest, 2022
Vivienne Shalom's *The Truth Is,* Winner of Jonathan Holden Poetry
    Chapbook Contest, 2023
Linda Enders, *Consider the Gravity*, Finalist of Jonathan Holden
    Poetry Chapbook Contest, 2023
Jane Wiseman's *Bee Telephone*, Winner of Jonathan Holden Poetry
    Chapbook Contest, 2024
Rochelle Germond's *Confessions of a Heliophiliac*, Finalist of
    Jonathan Holden Poetry Chapbook Contest, 2024
Cody Shrum's *Green Acre*, Finalist of Jonathan Holden Poetry
    Chapbook Contest, 2024
Christine Andersen's *To Maggie Wherever You've Gone*, Winner of
    Jonathan Holden Poetry Chapbook Contest, 2025

Nonfiction:
Jacquelyn Shah's *Limited Engagement*, Winner of the Kenneth
    Johnston Nonfiction Book Award, 2022
Tracy Robert's *Angora Panties*, Winner of the Kenneth Johnston
    Nonfiction Book Award, 2023
JoDean Nicolette's *Trail Magic*, Finalist of the Kenneth Johnston
    Nonfiction Book Award, 2023
Anna Redsand's *Crevice*, Winner of the Kenneth Johnston Nonfiction
    Book Award, 2024
Richard Holinger's *Manure Dreams*, Winner of the Kenneth Johnston
    Nonfiction Book Award, 2025

Fun Fact
Choeofpleirn
pronounced "chuf-plern"
is a combination of our
surnames by alternating
the letters
www.choeofpleirnpress.com

Choeofpleirn Press
www.choeofpleirnpress.com
choeofpleirnpress@gmail.com

Copyright © 2022

www.ingramcontent.com/pod-product-compliance
Lightning Source LLC
Chambersburg PA
CBHW040115150726
48005CB00013B/1726